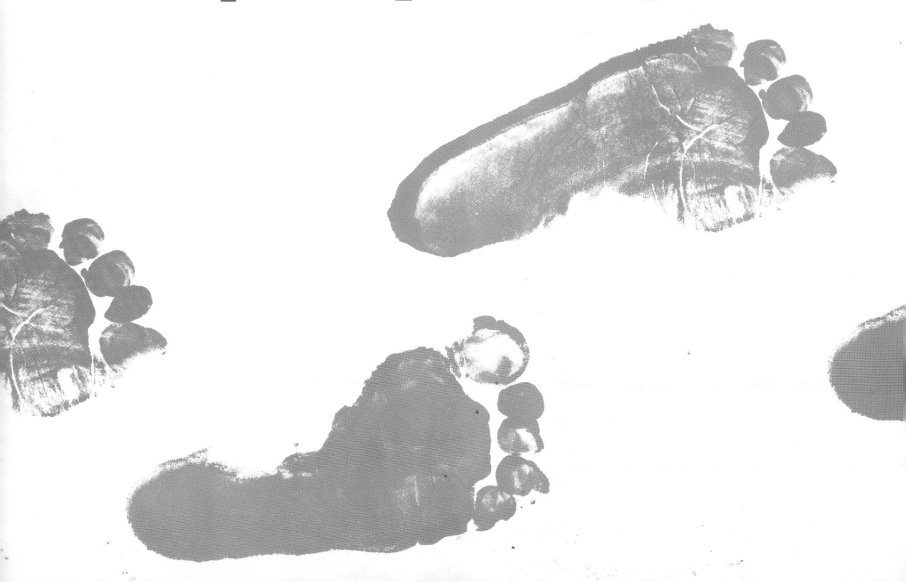

Step by Step

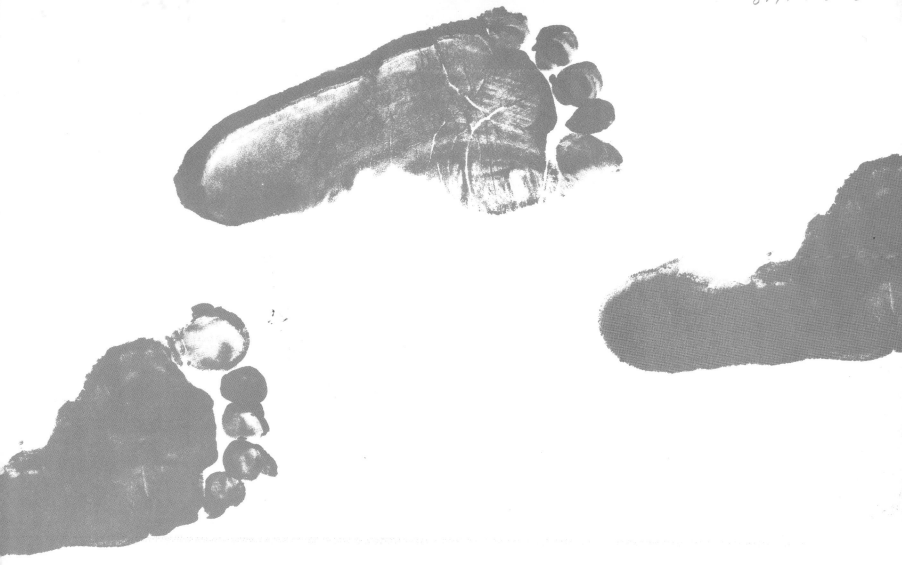

by Bruce McMillan

Lothrop, Lee & Shepard Books   New York

For Rick & Pat & Evan

First Edition 1 2 3 4 5 6 7 8 9 10

Library of Congress Cataloging in Publication Data
McMillan, Bruce. Step by step.
Summary: The author/photographer follows Evan with a camera for ten months and records his steps in learning to walk as Evan crawls, stands, climbs, walks, and runs. [1. Babies—Fiction. 2. Growth—Fiction] I. Title.
PZ7.M2278St 1987   [E]   87-4195
ISBN 0-688-07233-X   ISBN 0-688-07234-8 (lib. bdg.)

sleeping

waking

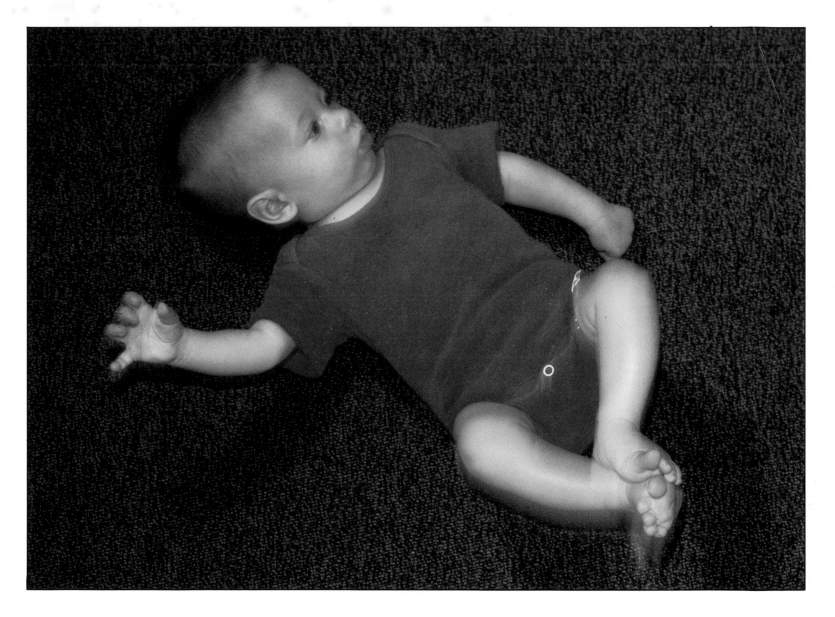

kicking

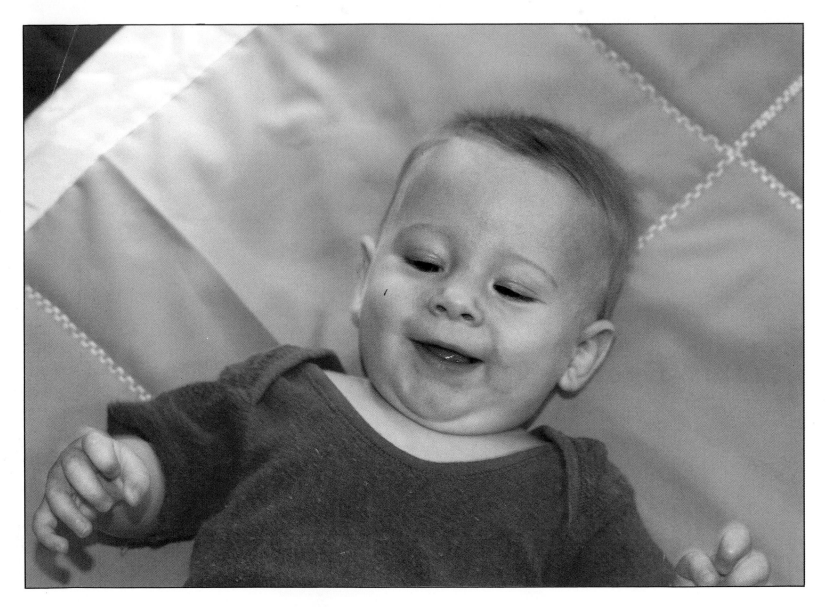

reaching

pushing up

rolling over

crawling

**kneeling
and
holding
on**

kneeling
and
letting
go

sitting

standing up

**holding
on**

stepping
away

looking in

tossing

looking out

climbing up

clapping

climbing down

walking

wading

running home

About This Book

Evan Corwine Kaye-Schiess was four months old when we began to photograph this book. I concentrated on capturing Evan's achievements in locomotion. The last group of photographs were taken when he was fourteen months old. In a sense, Evan himself wrote this book. One day, shortly after finishing the last photographs, I stopped by the Kaye-Schiess home to visit. Evan, who was lying on the floor, rolled over, pulled himself to his knees, stood up, took a step, and then ran to greet me. In a short five seconds, I saw the book—the progress that had taken Evan ten months to achieve—flash before my eyes.

The photographs were taken using Nikon F2 and FE2 motor-driven cameras, with 28, 35, 50, 105 and 200mm Nikkor lenses. The lighting was a mix of available light, bare bulb flash, multiple unit flash, and incandescent reflector floodlight. The film used was Kodachrome 64, processed by Eastman Kodak.

I wish to thank Evan's parents, Pat and Rick, for their friendship, as well as their help and cooperation.